DEAR LIZ

Lisa Andrews

DEAR LIZ
Lisa Andrews

© 2016 Lisa Andrews

Book design: kd diamond
Cover art: Katie Commodore

Published by Indolent Books,
an imprint of Indolent Enterprises, LLC

www.indolentbooks.com
Brooklyn, New York

ISBN: 978-1-945023-00-2

CONTENTS

What Prayer Is (In Which the Audience Is God) 9
Sparrow 10
July 4, 1979 11
Jones Beach 12
Summer 1979 14
No Future Then 15
Your Stories 16
That February in Chicago 17
California in Chicago 18
That Afternoon in the Park You Used the Past Tense 19
What I Didn't Tell You Then 20
What Weather Was Like 21
Advantages of Watching a Movie from 1944 at 3:00 in the Afternoon 22
Suspicion 25
Dear Liz 26
Writing You 27
Without End 28
Skating 29
The Dead Are So Invisible 30
Machine 31
I Can't Get Back 32
Lucent Machine 33
Deer Struck in Headlights 34

In memory of Elizabeth S. Roberts

And how can the dead be truly dead when they still live in the souls of those who are left behind?

—*Carson McCullers, The Heart Is a Lonely Hunter*

What Prayer Is
(In Which the Audience Is God)

I do not know how to pray, but I sometimes imagine
it might be like singing
for an audience that already knows

you can't sing, and so
you must do the impossible, considering
they've left their homes for this—

winter coats and scarves,
far better things to do than this
on such a cold night, only

for this exact and awkward moment,
even they have nothing better to do
than this: to hear you sing

in a voice they will teach you
to call your own—the one
they've come this far to hear.

Sparrow

That story we read in class one winter afternoon—
already dark outside—bare trees and windows,
and those small, hard desks at which we sat,
marveling at the story of the sparrow's swift flight
through the brightly lit banquet hall. I felt
something shiver—was it something already inside me,
or had it come from the story itself—
the chill of those words, their exquisite and brutal
shimmer—The light in that room *shimmered*. It was years
before we met—I couldn't have imagined you
as the sparrow. I'd sooner have seen you
as the hall itself—that brightly lit place
where everything happens, and the light—
it's how I see you now—as light itself: what remains.

July 4, 1979

We are on the West Side Highway.
It is long before the fireworks will start,
but we're young and will not mind the wait.

Being on a highway and walking
astonishes me (I am from Detroit).
I love that cars have been banished.

So many people on a highway,
all walking and no cars, and suddenly—
you are singing—the Star-Spangled Banner, no less—

and I—I admit it—cringe a little, afraid
how the crowd will react. Flocks of strangers around us—
singly and in couples, then groups—

begin to add their voices. Everyone ready for this, it seems,
waiting for it even, and soon, all the people,
the entire West Side Highway, now singing like you.

The highway a platform, a stage—the impossible theater of this.
I think MGM, Fred Astaire, Walt Whitman.
Something heroic, unstoppable—the music, you.

How you loved the world, and the world loved you back.
How if you felt like singing, you sang. How contagious it was.
That doing and no second-guessing—pure action and love.

We are young and never tired. We can wait forever
for the sun to set, for the fireworks to begin.

Jones Beach

The two of us in your father's car, boatlike and rolling—
the highway packed, the beach packed—
                                        so many bodies in the hot sun—
did we even swim?—all day that day,
failing to realize we were burning all that time.

Now back at your parents' house,
in an upstairs bathroom so clean
it can't possibly be meant for use,
                                        we find—
inside a glass jar on a glass shelf—
                                        aloe vera capsules—

each green and golden oval filled
with a liquid kind of summer light.
These will cool us off, you say.

Impossible to open—and so,
realizing what's needed, you leave and return
with supplies—two safety pins,

glistening and illicit. We go to work,
puncture each oval, squeeze
its slippery skin, until

the sticky substance inside
releases itself, mostly
                                        misses us, and splatters
over the immaculate tiles—
a riot of crushed and gutted skins.

                                      We can't stop
opening those ovals, endless and impossible
to hold still for one second, the oil sliding off
our skin, the greatest relief is in
                                        breaking open

the next and the next, thinking
each time, *this time,*
this one will cool us off.

We are opening—green and golden,
and there is no cooling off, not even
if I change this memory

                                          each time I open it.

Summer 1979

Skylab falling. The Allerton Hotel. Its curtains unfurling
over the traffic below—that all-night rush and hum.
I followed you everywhere that summer—

the entire length of Manhattan it seemed—always walking—
across 57th Street, up Broadway, down to Bleecker, then back.
A map of the city studded with movie theaters:

the Little Carnegie, the Regency, Embassy and Beacon.
The Bleecker Street Cinema, those nearby cafés,
where important smokers sipped their drinks.

Drunk on movies, two double features a day.
We are vehicles and this is our fuel: Clouzot, De Sica, Rossellini,
Truffaut, Kurosawa, and *The Muppet Movie*.

And always—Fred Astaire. Days in the dark,
our faces lit by those enormous screens,
the two of us never leaving until

the credits are done, the house lights up. And still,
we lingered there, as if over a threshold
we did not want to cross.

No Future Then

I swear there was no future then—
only each instant, a bead
that has no notion of a necklace.

No adding up, no cost or consequence,
no before or after, only
now and *now* and *now*—

The camera's ceaseless splendid flash:
This now, only *this—now*—
each instant separate and exact.

We lived inside a language
that had no future tense, only
the unadulterated present. Abundance

the thing that made it so invisible, the way
standing beneath a waterfall,
you are not likely to be thinking of thirst.

The future—almost scenic then,
a backdrop, something luxuriously in the distance—
you have yet to purchase the ticket—

something so far off—the place from which,
however improbably it might then have seemed,
I'm writing to you now.

Your Stories

I did not think the book of you would be done so soon.
I saw you as endless—multivolume, a set. You were the novel,
the book to which I could always turn, a story I could open
on any page, the way they say old friends can always continue
the conversation, pick up wherever they've left off, the way
that afternoon in the sudden rain, you welcomed us as if
you'd been expecting us all along, and the heavy rain
had been no accident at all, but a plot device, so that we
might sit by your fire and listen, as you told us your latest story—
screenplay, science fiction or script—back when all of us were young,
and I was almost careless in the driven rain.

That February in Chicago

All our doors and windows open—and you
so susceptible to cold (the chemo). I'd burned
the rice and pot. Smoke everywhere—and you

sat on the couch, putting on another coat and hat,
flexible and unfazed as any great actress
when all the props and scenery have gone awry.

You even took the garbage out that night.
(I'd sprained my elbow.) Who was taking care of whom,
I often wonder. And yet, it's your gratitude

I remember most, the way you noticed
how thinly I'd sliced the avocado. *It's hard*, you said,
when there's so little left to slice. And how glad you were
for that bowl of rice I'd left, when you'd said you weren't hungry.

California in Chicago

Remember how hard we laughed
when we heard that young woman say—
sliding into her skidding cab—snow
thick around its tires, luggage vanished, trunk slammed—
California! How it sounded
like a command: all destination now—all bliss, all snow.

                                        The snow was beautiful, and you
were in pain, cordoning it off as best you could,
determined to keep it in its place, keep it from taking over,
as long as any of it was in your power. The snow so beautiful,
I wouldn't call it, *the indifferent snow*. I'd call it,
oblivious snow. It had other things on its mind. It was snow
thinking of snow, being—like you—utterly itself.

A dome over us now. The present tense,
gated and embraced: oblivion and peace, and us—

That Afternoon in the Park You Used the Past Tense

I've loved my life, you said.
Even if I had had only one day on this earth,
it would have been worth it.
That was the day I realized. Not
that death might get the upper hand—
it never did, not really. That was the day
I knew and did not know, and in case
I didn't get it then, there was that time
at the hospital—all those doctors in your room,
a conference, your sister rushing out, giving me
such an enormous hug, and in case
I didn't get it then, there was that afternoon—
the hurricane now over, the lights finally on—
you told me there had been music that day,
how all the musicians had stayed in one place,
out of sight for most, out of hearing for many, and so,
we circled the ward, you, singing
in your unmistakable voice, singing
for all the people in all the rooms, you
with your IV pole like a staff, and I
holding some of the bags and lines—
the way I've seen small children
hold a wedding veil in a bride's wake, and in case
I didn't get it then, there was that Friday
I kissed your forehead and said, *I'll see you Sunday.*

What I Didn't Tell You Then

So many people in that room.
Why not say what matters most?

Outside, the rain is tender on the leaves.
The rain forgives the leaves, and the leaves

the rain. They have nothing to forgive
each other for. It's a ritual they go through.

September, walking up that slight hill,
my hand cupped beneath your elbow,

Good assist, you said. That's when I didn't say it.
And so, I am saying it now.

What Weather Was Like

Those two brackets, those hurricanes, the one
that was supposed to hit, and didn't, and the one
that brought the city to its knees. Hospitals evacuated,

businesses lost, homes washed away. Nothing working,
and everything stopped. Doctors, nurses, orderlies—
claiming all available couches, mattresses and beds.

Your husband sleeping on a set of three chairs—
all arms and no give. Your doctor
stuck at a hospital farther uptown.

Days later, walking from Brooklyn,
I saw how downtown looked—like something
not meant to be seen in the light. At the hospital—

tired people in white coats rushing off at the floor
where steel trolleys stood in the hall, shiny
with shrink-wrapped sandwiches on thin metal trays.

How when I got to your room, you said,
We watched the lights go out—as if everything external
were now happening through glass. The storm

a distraction or impediment—but not
the main event. Your gaze already beyond
the scope of that storm—and closer at hand:
your own green burial in the earth.

Advantages of Watching a Movie From 1944 at 3:00 in the Afternoon

1. I have not been born; therefore, none of my friends are sick, dead or in trouble.

2. If the movie ends, it can begin again. What I am watching has the illusion of a beginning, middle and end, but it's really a loop.

3. If the movie from 1944 is, say, two hours long, I know, in the last five minutes or so, what's likely to happen has to happen soon. There's only so much time.

4. In this movie, there are no insurance companies, no double billing, no dedicated service teams, no issue resolution experts, no hierarchy of obfuscation, inefficiency or cruelty.

5. No one inside this movie is going to correct my grammar, fire me, suggest I find another place to live.

6. No one inside this movie is going to call and call and put me in the position of not picking up for as long as the phone keeps ringing, because I know, without knowing, this is not a call I want to receive, and I actually think if I don't pick up the call, I can keep it from happening. The "it" cannot happen, will not happen, cannot have happened. Even if the caller hangs up and keeps calling back, I will not have to answer or willfully ignore this phone. If the phone rings, it's safe to assume it's not me they want.

7. Nothing I know can harm me now. Not here, not inside this movie. The movie is the preexisting condition, and we are the condition not yet in existence.

8. Nothing bad has happened yet.

9. Not that wind-knocked-out-of-you feeling; not that abrupt lack of desire for anything in the present or future tense—unimaginable state. No tears at inopportune moments—the airplane, the department store, the crosstown bus—the tears that are endless. The body, the heart, the mind would, if it could, cry forever.

10. Only, if I watch this movie from 1944, if I can somehow enter the movie, the way, for example, you could and did—could not help but enter each movie, pass through to the very inside—it means, even now (now that I, too, am inside this movie)—no matter that it is 1944—we are both alive.

11. It's a little like breakfast in childhood. No one is drinking yet; no one is screaming or crying—not at 7:00 a.m. Not in 1944.

12. I haven't met you yet or been born; therefore, you can't have died, are not now dead, especially since I don't think I ever really believed—apparently not—even when it should have been obvious—inescapable cold fact—not even then did I think you were dead. After all, I didn't see it. Not the end. Not with my own eyes.

13. But I've seen you enter a movie. And when you told your film professor you believed every movie was real, how whatever was happening on the screen was also happening to you, he said, *I'm afraid I can't help you with that*—which means you are inside the movie I am watching now, which means you are the movie I am watching.

14. I leave your phone numbers and address intact. I will not update, I will not delete. I will remember.

15. The way, in that hushed auditorium, you shouted, *Don't drink that glass of milk!* The way you stood in that theater in Times Square, announced: *I am Spartacus.*

16. If I watch a movie, then am I anywhere nearer? Are you?

17. When I see something I know you'd like to see, I lose control.

18. It's the opposite of the way a friend of mine, pregnant, would muse, when crossing the Brooklyn Bridge, *Oh, this is a view my child will one day see.* You see, it's like that, only in reverse.

19. But not with the movie from 1944. You could be sitting right here beside me, watching every frame. Even now. And if I watch what you have watched, am I not watching you? Am I not being watched by you?

Suspicion

I will always remember your warning,
shouted for all to hear, shouted as if

your voice alone could enter that world,
tear down walls, pierce celluloid—anything

to save that actress, keep her from drinking
that glass of milk, still glowing in the dark.

                    * * *

Sunday, the darkened auditorium, something
high above us in the back—its whir and hum,

dust motes in that hazy scream of light
from a window in the wall, an opening

so square, precise and prisonlike—light
pouring out in the shape of a megaphone—sound

from I don't know where or how, I only know
someone is climbing those stairs. I'm relying

on memory here, in which case,
Joan Fontaine is alive, and so, my friend, are you.

Dear Liz

The milk looks as radioactive as ever.
Only you could stop Joan Fontaine,

even as Cary Grant oh so slowly ascends
those carpeted stairs. Your warning works

every time. It's how I know
you're still here—somewhere close enough

that no matter how many times I see it, I know
she'll never drink that glass of milk.

Writing You

I didn't realize losing you would mean I'd never stop
missing you, here and now—this afternoon, for instance,
lunch at the Rubin Museum, the extra chair at my table—
Yes, the one where you are sitting.

You are here and not here, more real to me than these
melodious strangers, chatting in their dignified groups,
the music with its bells and chimes, soft clatter of keys
behind me, that solitary man staring at his screen.

You would want me to love the world, the train I took to get here,
its crowded stink and shove, sticky coke on the floor,
and a child whose shrieks were so piercing
I thought the train would stop in its tracks.

Without End

I thought death would have an end to it—I mean
for the living. What's more final than death? Humorless and flat—
no second chance, no taking back. Did I really imagine

some kind of letting go? Or that we would leave together,
as if for the theater, or some long, transatlantic flight?
Am I so in love with narrative—wedded

to a beginning, a middle, and an end? How could I not have known
how much the dead are with us—who if not us
to represent them on earth. We carry the dead—

not a weight but a light—inside us
no less than the past, our seemingly random
genetic code, memory and dust—

around us like saints or ghosts—
that light in the sky, bird in the branch, stranger up ahead,
the one who looks, just for one second, like you.

Skating

What do people do with all this love
after the fact. We are, all of us on earth,
                                        after the fact.

Like stargazers who stare at a single star—
all that light coming back
from its now dead source. That light—
                                a gift we took too long to receive.
We are so slow and late . . .

Whatever I am writing you, surely
you have already read, written yourself.
                                          I am skating

over your tracks. Grateful then—

to be spared the clean ice, given
the snow-dusted kind, cuts and marks all over it—
                                                  wanting to be steadied
by the tracks of those who have gone before.

The Dead Are So Invisible

The dead are so invisible—no matter how deeply felt
their absence is—their presence, so resolutely denied us.

It's almost boring really—how invisible they are—
like some childhood game, *Come out, Come out, Wherever you are.*

The dead are it. No, *we* are it—and this
the coldest game of hard to get. And still

we chase them, want them to save us,
come back for us—no matter the dead

have other things on their minds—
and who can say what *mind* might stand for?

Surely the dead are not so preoccupied with the living.
No one wants that, do they? And yet,

who if not us will they come back for? And how else
will we know how to find them?

Machine

In the dream there was a machine for visiting the dead, only
you needed to connect at the exact same time—if not,
the machinery would falter—gears slip and grind,
and the picture would waver and fail—the connection
so brief, a little like being on a high-speed train—
in the opposite direction, another train flashing past—
impossible to see anything at speeds like this, and yet—
if you are fast enough, want this badly enough—and here
perhaps even time slows down, lengthens itself—so that you
might catch the other person's face, and the other person
might possibly catch yours—for one second—
one glimpse—and each of you would see
not only the other, but also the other looking back:
the seeing and the being seen. *I was not invisible to you.*

I Can't Get Back

You and I were young and together, which is to say,
we were in the past—a college campus, half familiar
buildings and people, the same narrow paths, and even,

a phone call from you inside the dream—a message
I know I received, but waking can no longer remember.
I only know I had it—the dream, your words—

locked against me and lost, even as I tried to fall back asleep,
reenter the darkened theater I'd only just left for an instant, assuming
I could pick up where I'd left off, the same movie still playing.

As impossible now to reenter that dream
as it would be to have a conversation with the dead—
which is what these poems are, and are not.

Lucent Machine

I don't know who left it or why—
this message on a Friday in the middle of the day.
Not the usual 8:00 a.m. hang up. Not Citibank
Identity Theft Solutions. Not Capital One
still calling with an offer. No wrong number
about a change in an appointment—not mine.
No survey. No one asking for money or my vote.
No one telling me the car is outside. No one asking
about a sign in our yard. No solvable mystery—
not like the friend who called as the Easter Bunny—
a mystery it took us years to solve.

No record under "calls received"—
not "private caller" or "caller unknown"—
not even "out of area." No record at all.
Only this voice—a woman singing, then whistling—a voice
barely embodied by breath—hypnotic and jazzy
and pulling me in—this bluesy lullaby from beyond—
drowning in static and taking its time—
the only recognizable words—*sometime* and *goodbye*—
a voice so close to the one I keep telling myself
it can't possibly be.

Deer Struck in Headlights

We are deer, dumbstruck
in who knows whose headlights,
whose foot on the gas or brake,
whose visibility is poor,
who among us did not
see it coming, but felt
for years after
that drag and pull,
beneath us, over us—
call it love or death—
we're drowning in it—unquenchable
passion—even in death.

ACKNOWLEDGMENTS

These poems originally appeared, sometimes in different versions, in the following publications.

Painted Bride Quarterly: "Advantages of Watching a Movie From 1944 at 3:00 in the Afternoon"
HIV Here & Now: "Your Stories"

My great thanks to Michael Broder for his interest in the first place, his patience to the last, and for his astounding lack of indolence throughout. My thanks to kd diamond, Justin Alves, Casey Edwards, Katie Commodore, and to all the poets at Indolent Books. My thanks as well to 61 Local for all their hospitality. My thanks especially to Nancy Slonim Aronie and the group at Omega, where many of these poems began. I am indebted to Frankie Drayus and Sharon Kraus for their close reading of this manuscript, for their generosity and advice. My thanks to Peggy Wallin-Hart and Lucy Simic for their encouragement. To all my teachers and friends who have helped in so many ways—my thanks. And always, my thanks to my husband Tony Geiger—for his keen eye and ear—for everything.

ABOUT THE AUTHOR

Lisa Andrews grew up in Michigan and moved back to her native New York to study acting at the Neighborhood Playhouse School of the Theatre. A graduate of Hunter College, she received an MA in English Literature and an MFA in Poetry from NYU, where she taught in the Expository Writing Program and worked with poetry students at Goldwater Hospital and Bayview Correctional Facility. Chosen by Dael Orlandersmith as a recipient of the New Voice Poetry Award from the Writer's Voice of the West Side YMCA, Lisa has had residencies at Blue Mountain Center, the Virginia Center for the Creative Arts, and the Vermont Studio Center. Her poems have appeared in *Gargoyle, HIV Here & Now, Mudfish, Painted Bride Quarterly,* and *Zone 3.* She lives in Brooklyn, N.Y., with her husband, artist Tony Geiger.

ABOUT INDOLENT BOOKS

Indolent Books is a small independent press founded in 2015 and operating in Brooklyn. Indolent was founded as a home for poets of a certain age who have done the creative work but for whatever reason (family, career, self—effacement, etc.) have not published a first collection. But we are not dogmatic about that mission: Ultimately, we publish books we like and care about, short or long, poetry or prose. We are queer owned, queer staffed, and maintain a commitment to diversity among our authors, artists, designers, developers, and other team members.

www.ingramcontent.com/pod-product-compliance
Lightning Source LLC
Chambersburg PA
CBHW021454080526
44588CB00009B/846